D0627285

The Pebble® First Guide to

Butterflies

by Lori Shores

Consulting Editor: Gail Saunders-Smith, PhD

Consultant: Laura Jesse
Iowa State University
Plant and Insect Diagnostic Clinic
Ames, Iowa

Capstone press®

Mankato, Minnesota

Pebble Books are published by Capstone Press,
151 Good Counsel Drive, P.O. Box 669, Mankato, Minnesota 56002.
www.capstonepress.com

Copyright © 2009 by Capstone Press, a Capstone Publishers company.
All rights reserved. No part of this publication may be reproduced in whole
or in part, or stored in a retrieval system, or transmitted in any form or by any
means, electronic, mechanical, photocopying, recording, or otherwise,
without written permission of the publisher.
For information regarding permission, write to Capstone Press,
151 Good Counsel Drive, P.O. Box 669, Dept. R, Mankato, Minnesota 56002.
Printed in the United States of America

1 2 3 4 5 6 14 13 12 11 10 09

Library of Congress Cataloging-in-Publication Data
Shores, Lori.
    The Pebble first guide to butterflies / by Lori Shores; consulting editor,
Gail Saunders-Smith.
        p. cm. — (Pebble books. Pebble first guides)
    Includes bibliographical references and index.
    Summary: "A basic field guide format introduces 13 butterflies. Includes color
photographs and range maps" — Provided by publisher.
        ISBN-13: 978-1-4296-2241-7 (hardcover)   ISBN-10: 1-4296-2241-5 (hardcover)
        ISBN-13: 978-1-4296-3439-7 (paperback)   ISBN-10: 1-4296-3439-1 (paperback)
        1. Butterflies — Juvenile literature. I. Saunders-Smith, Gail. II. Title.
QL544.2.S49 2009
595.78'9 — dc22   2008028234

About Butterflies

This book features butterflies from eight of the nine chief butterfly families. All butterflies go through a life cycle that involves a series of stages called metamorphosis. The second stage of a butterfly's life cycle is larva or caterpillar.

Note to Parents and Teachers

The Pebble First Guides set supports science standards related to life science. In a reference format, this book describes and illustrates 13 butterflies. This book introduces early readers to subject-specific vocabulary words, which are defined in the Glossary section. Early readers may need assistance to read some words and to use the Table of Contents, Glossary, Read More, Internet Sites, and Index sections of the book.

Table of Contents

American Snout 4

Cabbage White 6

Common Roadside-Skipper 8

Giant Swallowtail 10

Great Purple Hairstreak 12

Great Spangled Fritillary 14

Little Wood Satyr 16

Monarch 18

Mourningcloak 20

Orange Sulphur 22

Painted Lady 24

Queen Alexandra's Birdwing 26

Red Admiral 28

Glossary 30

Read More 31

Internet Sites 31

Index 32

snout

Wingspan:	1.5 to 2 inches (3.8 to 5 centimeters)
Adult food:	nectar from dogbane, goldenrod, and other flowers
Caterpillar food:	hackberry leaves
Lives:	prairies, open areas, forests
Facts:	• mouthparts form a snout on adults
	• sometimes live in groups of millions

American Snout Range

☐ North America, Central America, Caribbean islands, South America

caterpillar

Cabbage White

male

female

Wingspan:	1.2 to 2.25 inches (3 to 5.7 centimeters)
Adult food:	flower nectar
Caterpillar food:	cabbage, broccoli, brussels sprouts
Lives:	farmland, city gardens
Facts:	• female has two black spots on wings • brought to North America from Europe in 1860s

Cabbage White Range

☐ North America, Europe,
southern Asia, Australia

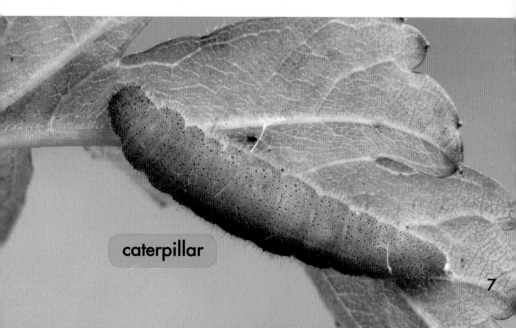

caterpillar

Wingspan:	⅞ to 1 inch (2.2 to 2.5 centimeters)
Adult food:	nectar from verbena and other flowers
Caterpillar food:	wild oats and other grasses
Lives:	forests, prairies, open areas
Facts:	• flies fast
	• stays close to the ground

Common Roadside-Skipper Range

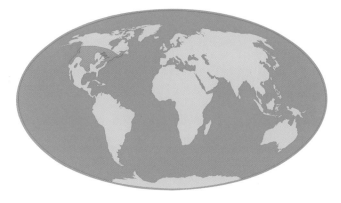

■ North America

Giant Swallowtail

Wingspan:	3.75 to 5.5 inches (9.5 to 14 centimeters)
Adult food:	nectar from azalea, orange blossoms, and other flowers
Caterpillar food:	wild plants, citrus plants, prickly ash
Lives:	prairies, open areas, forests, farmland
Facts:	• name comes from "tails" on back wings
	• caterpillars look like bird droppings

Giant Swallowtail Range

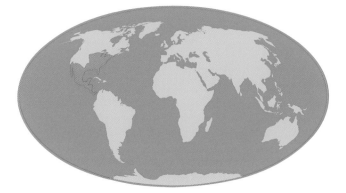

■ southern and eastern North America, Central America

caterpillar

Wingspan:	1.25 to 2 inches (3 to 5 centimeters)
Adult food:	nectar from goldenrod and other flowers
Caterpillar food:	mistletoe
Lives:	forests, prairies, open areas
Facts:	• underside of body is bright red
	• has two long tails on back wings

12

Great Purple Hairstreak Range

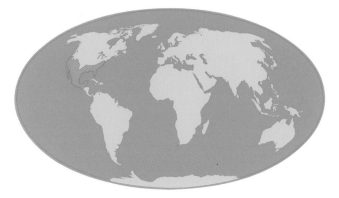

☐ southern North America, Central America

caterpillar

13

Wingspan:	2.5 to 3.5 inches (6.4 to 8.9 centimeters)
Adult food:	nectar from milkweed, thistles, and other flowers
Caterpillar food:	violets
Lives:	meadows, prairies, open areas
Facts:	• can be light or dark orange • caterpillars hide under dead leaves in winter

14

Great Spangled Fritillary Range

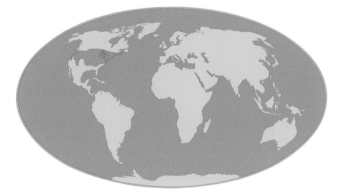

☐ southern Canada to southern United States

caterpillar

Wingspan:	1.5 to 2 inches (3.8 to 5 centimeters)
Adult food:	sap, rotten fruit
Caterpillar food:	grasses
Lives:	prairies, open areas, forests
Facts:	• slow, bouncing flight
	• flies low to the ground

Little Wood Satyr Range

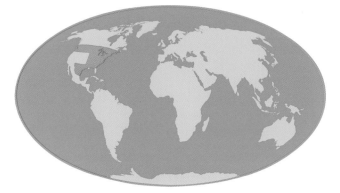

■ southern Canada, eastern United States, northeastern Mexico

chrysalis

Wingspan:	3.5 to 4.9 inches (8.9 to 12.4 centimeters)
Adult food:	nectar from milkweed, dogbane, and other flowers
Caterpillar food:	milkweed
Lives:	prairies, open areas, farmland
Facts:	• orange and black markings show it is poisonous to predators
	• spends winter in trees in large groups

18

Monarch Range

■ North America, Central America, South America, southern Asia, Australia

caterpillar

Mourningcloak

Wingspan: 2.25 to 4 inches (5.7 to 10 centimeters)

Adult food: oak tree sap, rotting fruit

Caterpillar food: willow, poplar, elm, and birch tree leaves

Lives: prairies, open areas, forests, mountains

Facts:
- adults can live up to 10 months
- called the Camberwell Beauty in England

Mourningcloak Range

☐ North America, Europe, southern Asia

caterpillar

Wingspan:	1.5 to 2.5 inches (3.8 to 6.4 centimeters)
Adult food:	dandelions, milkweed, goldenrod, aster
Caterpillar food:	alfalfa, clover
Lives:	prairies, open areas, farmland
Facts:	• most often seen feeding on flowers • also called alfalfa sulphur

Orange Sulphur Range

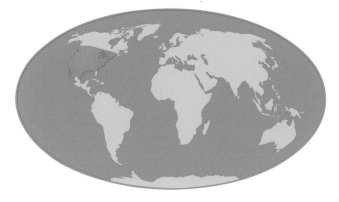

⬛ North America

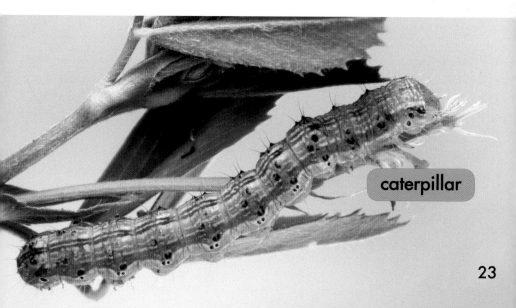

caterpillar

Painted Lady

Wingspan:	2 to 2.5 inches (5 to 6.4 centimeters)
Adult food:	nectar from thistles and other flowers
Caterpillar food:	thistles, mallows
Lives:	prairies, open areas
Facts:	• migrates north each summer • also called thistle butterfly

Painted Lady Range

☐ worldwide, except Australia and Antarctica

caterpillar

25

Queen Alexandra's Birdwing

male

female

Wingspan: 6.75 to 11 inches
(17 to 28 centimeters)

Adult food: flower nectar

Caterpillar food: pipe vine leaves

Lives: rain forests

Facts:
- largest known butterfly
- endangered

Queen Alexandra's Birdwing Range

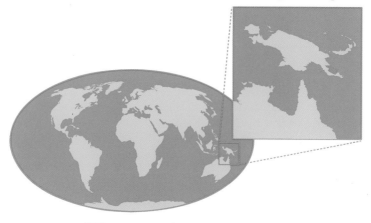

☐ Papua New Guinea

caterpillar

Wingspan:	2 to 2.5 inches (5 to 6.4 centimeters)
Adult food:	tree sap, rotten fruit, liquid on bird droppings
Caterpillar food:	nettles
Lives:	prairies, open areas, forests, farmland, gardens
Facts:	• sips nectar if there is no other food
	• strong wings help it fly long distances

Red Admiral Range

☐ North America, Central America, northern Africa, Europe, Asia

caterpillar

Glossary

caterpillar — a larva that changes into a butterfly or moth; a caterpillar is the second life stage of a butterfly.

chrysalis — the third stage of a butterfly; pupa is another word for chrysalis.

dropping — bird waste

endangered — at risk of dying out

migrate — to move from one place to another

nectar — a sweet liquid that some insects collect from flowers and eat as food

poisonous — able to harm or kill with poison or venom

prairie — a large area of flat or rolling grassland with few or no trees

sap — a fluid found inside plants and trees

wingspan — the distance between the tips of a pair of wings when fully open

Read More

Ling, Mary. *Butterfly*. See How They Grow. New York: DK, 2007.

Stewart, Melissa. *My Butterfly Book*. New York: Collins, 2008.

Internet Sites

FactHound offers a safe, fun way to find educator-approved Internet sites related to this book.

Here's what you do:

1. Visit *www.facthound.com*

2. Choose your grade level.

3. Begin your search.

This book's ID number is 9781429622417.

FactHound will fetch the best sites for you!

Index

bodies, 12
caterpillars, 10, 14
coloring, 6, 12, 14, 18
endangered, 26
farmland, 6, 10, 18,
     22, 28
flight, 8, 16, 28
forests, 4, 8, 10, 12, 16,
     20, 28

gardens, 6, 28
groups, 4, 18
lifespan, 20
migrating, 24
nectar, 4, 6, 8, 10, 12,
     14, 18, 24, 26, 28
poisonous, 18
rain forests, 26
wings, 6, 10, 12, 28

Grade: 1
Early-Intervention Level: 22

Editorial Credits
Katy Kudela, editor; Alison Thiele, set designer; Biner Design, book designer;
     Jo Miller, photo researcher

Photo Credits
Alamy/Clint Farlinger, 17 (right); James Urbach, 12; Rick & Nora Bowers, 4, 5, 8, 9,
     13, 16, 17 (left)
Bruce Coleman Inc./Bob Jensen; 23, John P. Marechal, 21; Phyllis Betow, 15
Capstone Press/Karon Dubke, cover (monarch), 18 (both), 19, 24, 25
Getty Images Inc./Minden Pictures/Cisca Castelijns/Foto Natura, 7
iStockphoto/Dianne Maire, 6 (right)
James P. Rowan, 10
Pete Carmichael, 11
Peter Arnold/Biosphoto/BIOS/Gilson Francois, 26, 27; Wildlife, 29
Shutterstock/Claudia Steininger, 28; Jens Stolt, 20; Kerioak - Christine Nichols, cover
     (cabbage white); Lena Grottling, cover (giant swallowtail); Sergey Chushkin, 6 (left);
     Steve Byland, 14; Steve McWilliam, cover (red admiral)
Visuals Unlimited/Barbara Gerlach, 22

CANCELLED

Westlake Porter Library
Westlake, OH 44145